FREDDIE THE FROG®

STICKS!

BUILDING MATH & MUSIC CONNECTIONS

BY
SHARON BURCH

Freddie the Frog® and the incredible Centerville kids

DIGITAL DOWNLOAD CODE
To access digital content go to:
www.halleonard.com/mylibrary

Enter Code
3068-2677-1544-9647

Illustrations by Wilma Sanchez

ISBN 978-1-4803-4266-8

SHAWNEE PRESS

EXCLUSIVELY DISTRIBUTED BY

HAL•LEONARD®

7777 W. BLUEMOUND RD. P.O. BOX 13819 MILWAUKEE, WI 53213

Visit Hal Leonard Online at
www.halleonard.com

Visit Shawnee Press Online at
www.shawneepress.com

Contact Us:
Hal Leonard
7777 West Bluemound Road
Milwaukee, WI 53213
Email: info@halleonard.com

In Europe contact:
Hal Leonard Europe Limited
42 Wigmore Street
Marylebone, London, W1U 2RN
Email: info@halleonardeurope.com

In Australia contact:
Hal Leonard Australia Pty. Ltd.
4 Lentara Court
Cheltenham, Victoria, 3192 Australia
Email: info@halleonard.com.au

TABLE OF CONTENTS

INTRODUCTION

Children in kindergarten through second grade can easily compose, read, and play simple 4-beat rhythm patterns using craft sticks. This teacher's guide will lead you through the steps of teaching basic rhythm notation and patterns, reading simple solfeggio songs, and composition – all using craft sticks. As an added bonus, students learn common core math concepts in the process! It is an easy way to incorporate the Common Core State Math Standards in your music classroom while teaching music notation. Your principal will be thrilled!

Simply follow the steps outlined in this book. Each step leads to something fun for the kids to sing or play, keeping the students excited and engaged in the learning and fun to that last second of class.

Enjoy!

Sharon Burch
Elementary Music Specialist
Creator of **FREDDIE THE FROG**® Books

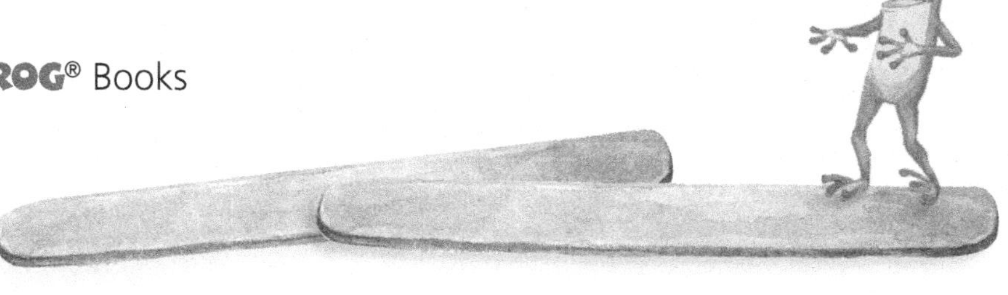

Sharon Burch is a National Board Certified Teacher in Early and Middle Childhood Music, a certified teacher with the International Piano Teaching Foundation, and holds a master's degree as a Professional Educator. Teaching creatively, Sharon introduced Freddie the Frog® to her classroom of music students and discovered the magic of games, storytelling and puppetry in teaching. She authored *Freddie the Frog and the Thump in the Night*, *Freddie the Frog and the Bass Clef Monster, Freddie the Frog and the Mysterious Wahooooo,* and *Freddie the Frog and the Secret of Crater Island* as the first of several adventuresome stories introducing fundamental music concepts. *Freddie the Frog and the Flying Jazz Kitten* introduces jazz through scat and improvisation. Teachers and children around the world love Freddie the Frog.® Sharon serves on the national Jazz Education Network Elementary Jazz Committee and enjoys sharing her teaching strategies and processes at music conferences and clinics with teachers around the globe.

A FOUNDATION FOR CRAFT STICKS

1. STORYBOOK INTRODUCTION

Freddie the Frog® and the Mysterious Wahooooo
Book/Audio CD
Written by Sharon Burch
Illustrated by Tiffany Harris

Freddie the Frog® and the Mysterious Wahooooo introduces kids to recognizing simple rhythm patterns, different tempo terms, and feeling the beat. It also lays the foundation for using *Sticks!*

2. MAGNETIC RHYTHM BOARD SET

- Chant and play the rhythm on the magnet board.
- Have one student choose a magnet to place on one of the four marked counts on the magnet board.
- Chant the new rhythm pattern, repeating the rhythm until it is changed again.
- The rhythm board is a great assessment tool and perfect for composing four-count rhythm patterns, preparing students to create their own patterns using craft sticks.

SOLD SEPARATELY

An online magnetic rhythm board is available at:
www.FreddieTheFrog.com

3. CRAFT STICK RHYTHM NOTATION

Since the birds use sticks to create rhythm patterns in the *Mysterious Wahooooo* book and on the magnetic rhythm board, it is easy for students to create their own rhythm patterns using craft sticks.

TEACHERS' NOTE

Don't tell, ask. For ultimate learning, ask questions and lead the students in the thinking process.

Ask the students to count out six sticks. To begin incorporating math concepts, you may choose to ask the following questions while teaching the concepts below.

4. QUARTER NOTE (TA)

"How many sticks does it take to make a 'ta'?"
(Answer: 1)

5. TWO EIGHTH NOTES (TI-TI)

"How many sticks does it take to make a 'ti-ti'?"
(Answer: 3)

6. FOUR SIXTEENTH NOTES (TIKA-TIKA)

"How many sticks does it take to make a 'tika-tika'?"
(Answer: 6)

To build the sixteenth notes, have students add two sticks vertically up and down inside the ti-ti. Then add an additional stick across the top horizontally.

7. QUARTER REST (SHH)

"How many sticks does it take to make a 'shh?'"
(Answer: 3)

MATH CONCEPTS IN THE MUSIC LESSON

CRAFT STICK 4-BEAT PATTERNS

Using sticks to create rhythm patterns provides a great opportunity to introduce algebra, counting, patterns, and other math concepts. *(See Appendix A: Math and Music.)*

Rhythm patterns are full of patterns, thus the name. The following steps can be used all within one class period if it is an older group, or broken down to a few steps at a time per class for a younger group.

COMMON CORE STANDARDS

K-3 MATHEMATICS

ASKING THE RIGHT QUESTIONS

Asking the students the right questions is an essential part of the learning process. Questions are the easiest way to incorporate the Common Core Standards in the area of K-3 Mathematics while teaching music. Students are more engaged in every moment of the lesson when questions are used in the process.

Pages 7–12 include questions to model that incorporate Common Core Standards in Math, and elicit higher-order thinking and creative processing. A detailed list of the Common Core Standards in the area of K-3 Mathematics met with the activities in this book are located in Appendix A.

THE FIRST CRAFT STICK PATTERN

- **"How many 'things' will there be in a pattern?"** *(Answer: 4)*
  Using *Freddie the Frog® and the Mysterious Wahooooo* as a guide, they will answer "four." Obviously, there are many different amounts that you could have, but to keep it simple I start with a base of always having four things, or four counts, in a rhythm pattern. Exceptions will come later.

TEACHERS' NOTE

Say "things" rather than "counts."

Using the word "counts" automatically means counting and that is confusing when you're holding a bunch of sticks in your hands and talking about counting in the general classroom. It is less confusing to use the word "things," as in "four things in a rhythm pattern." If you say how many "things" and point to a rhythm pattern in the book, they quickly can see the four different "things," which we know as counts or beats.

- **"How can I make a 'ta, ta, ti-ti, ta' rhythm pattern with sticks?"** Ask a student volunteer to come to the front and create the pattern for the class.
- **"How many sticks does it take to make the 'ta, ta, ti-ti, ta' rhythm pattern?"** (Answer: 6)
- Arrange the students in a circle or long lines, if possible.
- Place piles of sticks in front of groups of kids and ask them to count out six sticks and recreate the same "ta, ta, ti-ti, ta" rhythm pattern.
- Quickly glance to assess successful task completion.
- Ask the students to use their index finger and chant the pattern together, following along on their own pattern from left to right.
- Repeat chanting and pointing until you ask them to stop. This gives you time to assess and assist individuals.

TEACHERS' NOTE

Visually assess any students that need additional help, and give silent, individual help by pointing with them as the class chants the rhythm pattern. This task also helps reinforce the skill of reading left to right.

- Have your students make another rhythm pattern with four "things" in it using six sticks. It cannot be the same as their neighbor's pattern.
- Point to the first student's pattern and have the student point to and chant it; have the other students echo. Move to the next student in line and do the same thing, all while keeping a continuous beat until you've finished with the last student. Add rhythm instruments and repeat if desired.

IN THIS PHOTO, STUDENTS MADE A 4-COUNT PATTERN WITH ANY NUMBER OF STICKS

STICK LESSON EXTENSIONS AND VARIATIONS:

- Add a largo, andante, or allegro tempo track from the Mysterious Wahoooooo CD. This CD is perfect to accompany the class rhythm pattern piece as it is chanted and played with non-pitched classroom instruments.
- Create new rhythm patterns.
- Add more sticks for new patterns.
- Create AB measure patterns with the four-count rhythm patterns. In AB patterns, every other rhythm pattern is identical. Have students chant the progression as they did before, but this time they will hear the recurring pattern and it will begin to sound more like a real piece to them rather than unending changing rhythms.

- **Ask "Does anyone recognize a pattern?"** *(Answer: AB pattern)* Discuss how the patterns make it sound more like a piece of music.
- **"What other measure patterns could we create?"** *(Answer: ABA, ABACA, etc.)* The creative possibilities are endless!

TEACHERS' NOTE

It is essential to use these stick lessons before introducing the Sticks Sequence on the next page.

THE STICKS SEQUENCE

STEP 1. PLAY THE GAME

Play one of the games outlined in this book (starting on page 14) any day prior to introducing the correlating written Mystery Song.

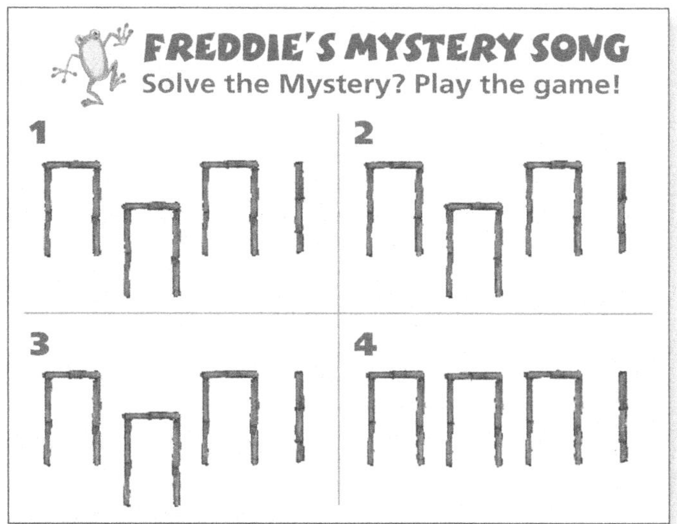

STEP 2. SOLVE THE MYSTERY SONG

Before the students enter the room, draw four rectangles on the board as shown here. Each rectangle represents a measure. Number each rectangle 1-4. Lead the students to "solve the mystery." Details on how to do this are on the next page. They get to play the game when the mystery is solved!

STEP 3. CRAFT STICK LESSON

Implement the stick activity as suggested with each singing game.

STEP 4. PLAY THE GAME...AGAIN

Play the game as described or with one of the variations, depending on the age and ability of the class.

Follow these four steps each time.
Different types of music learning and processing happen at each step.

HOW TO INTRODUCE A MYSTERY SONG

TEACHERS' NOTE

Establish the "Solve the Mystery Song" routine the first time you introduce the activity to the students. Once established, the students will be trained so when they see "Solve the Mystery? Play the Game!" on the board, they'll already know what to do and will silently go to their assigned seat and try to solve the mystery inside their head. Solving the mystery song to "get to" play the game makes practicing audiation relevant to kids.

- **Why is this important?**
  - Great for classroom management.
  - Developing audiation is part of developing great musicians with a high-level thought process of mentally hearing and comprehending music, even when no physical sound is present.

Before the students enter the room, draw four rectangles on the board as shown below. Each rectangle represents a measure. Number each rectangle 1-4. Draw as shown or use the PDF or PPT file included via Digital Access. Easily import the JPG files into your interactive whiteboard resource library.

Introduce the mystery song the first time by pointing it out on the board and telling them if they can solve it, they get to play the game. To guide them in solving the mystery, follow the steps below.

1. Ask your students to chant the rhythm beginning in box 1.
2. Ask the students if they see a pattern.
   - "Which boxes are the same?" (Answer: 1, 2 & 3)
   - "Which box is different?" *(Answer: 4)* "Why?"

3. "There are special singing words that help us learn the melody."
   - Demonstrate that the first two notes are "sol" and write an "s" under each of them.
   - The third and fourth notes are "mi", so write an "m" under each.
4. Demonstrate singing "sol-sol, mi-mi." Have your students echo.
5. "What letter should you write under notes 5 & 6?" *(Answer: "s" for sol)*
6. "Can you finish telling me what letters to put underneath each note?"
7. Echo-sing each box if this is the students' first experience with solfege.
8. "Can anyone can sing it alone?" Give students a chance to try singing it all the way through on their own before hearing you sing it all the way through.
9. Have the entire class sing the song in solfege without your help. Once it is sung successfully, you are ready for the last step.
10. "Does anyone recognize this singing game? Can you tell me the lyrics, or the real words?" Guide students to the answer if they need help.
11. Sing the lyrics and move to the stick activity or play the game, depending on which works best for that particular game. (For example, "Engine, Engine" works best to play the game and then get out the sticks because the students are organized in small circles at the end of the game.)

Use a similar sequence to introduce each mystery song, adapting notation and questioning for each specific song.

WHY RECTANGLE BOX MEASURES?

When primary students begin to read rhythm patterns, the "ta" (quarter note) is typically a single vertical line. When we draw measures of music on the board using "ta," "ti-ti," and bar lines, the bar lines can become confusing and the kids often have difficulty knowing if it is a "ta" or a bar line.

- Use rectangular boxes because they look similar to flash cards with rhythm patterns.
- Once the students are comfortable with the rectangular boxes and how many things go in each box, demonstrate that you can just draw the bar line instead of drawing the entire rectangular box and it means the same thing. Because they've used boxes for so long, switching to just one line is no longer confusing when used with a quarter note.
- This saves you a lot of time and headache.

Math and music learning abound in every stick activity. Again, lead the students into discovery learning and higher-order thinking through asking questions rather than simply telling them what to do.

SOL MI MYSTERY SONGS

1. ENGINE, ENGINE
2. CHOO CHOO TRAIN
3. PUMPKIN FAT
4. HILL, HILL
5. LEMONADE
6. NO ROBBERS OUT TODAY

ENGINE, ENGINE

GAME

Choose a group of 4 or 5 to demonstrate the game the first time you play it. After students understand the game, divide the class into equal-numbered groups.

1. Students in each group stand in a circle. Each person holds both fists in front.

2. One person is the "conductor." The conductor moves around the circle tapping the tops of the other students' fists in sequence. Whoever is tapped on the last word of the song is the next "conductor."
3. The "conductor" who just finished places his or her fists behind his or her back, or plays a rhythm instrument to the beat, while the rest of the circle continues to play.
4. The last student to be tapped who has not been a "conductor" moves to a new circle of students and is the first "conductor" of the new group. Begin the game again with the new circles.

TEACHERS' NOTE

Organize the small circles around the perimeter of the room. Establish a rotation pattern, such as each new conductor moves clockwise to the next small circle.

Display 1: Rhythm only.

Display 2: Add solfege hint.

Display 3: Add solfege.

Display 4: Add lyrics.

STICKS ACTIVITY:
ENGINE, ENGINE

1. Adjust the small circles to groups of four.
2. Have students "count off" 1-4, so each student in the group has a number in sequential order. Place piles of sticks in the center of each circle and instruct each student to count out the number of sticks needed to notate their assigned box. If this is the first time, demonstrate with one group first for clarity, then complete the activity with the whole class.
3. Have the students use the sticks to "notate" their assigned box, or measure, of the Mystery Song on the board. Be sure to ask leading questions to help them complete the task.
   - "How many sticks will it take to notate box 1?" *(Answer: 10)*
   - Continue the questioning with box 2, 3, and 4. As they answer, each member of the group notates their box (measure) with the craft sticks on the floor.
   - Include questions such as "Which boxes are alike?" and "Which are different?" for better understanding.
4. Sing the song while student 1 points to the first beat of his or her measure and moves finger left to right with the beat; student 2 takes over on his or her measure, then #3, and finally #4. Repeat until you observe that every circle has successfully notated the correct rhythms and they are pointing to the rhythms correctly.

TEACHER'S NOTE

Repetition allows time to silently help any individual or group while the class is actively engaged in singing and following the stick notation with their fingers. Encourage peer teaching and teamwork within groups.

CHOO CHOO TRAIN

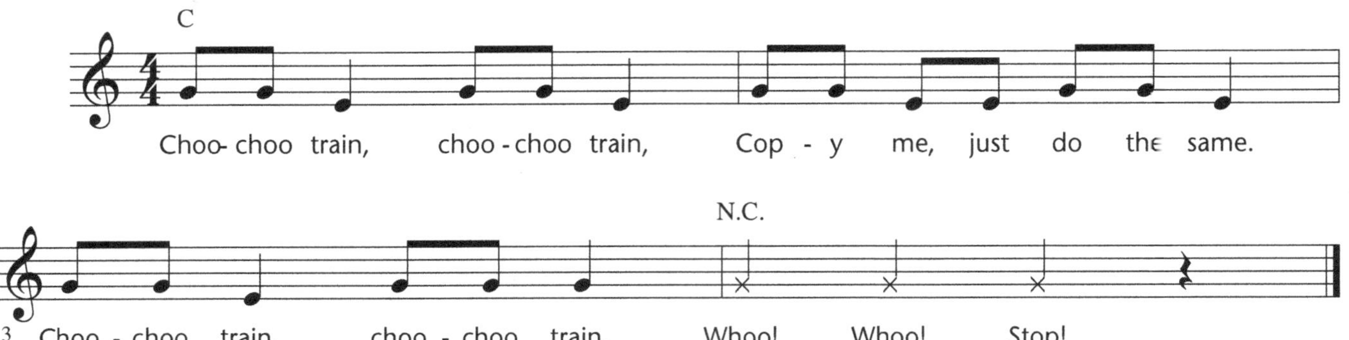

GAME

Students stand in a line, ready to follow the leader, with their arms bent at a right angle from the elbow. Practice "train-chugging arms" by having the students move their bent arms forward and back in small circles. The student who was first to solve the mystery song gets to be the first "conductor" of the train of students.

1. In measure 1, the train of students begins to move, chugging their arms and following the leader/conductor.
2. In measure 2, the conductor chooses a tapping movement on their body while singing the lyrics as a solo.
3. In measure 3, the rest of the train copies beat-tapping movements of the conductor.
4. In measure 4, everyone reaches up to "pull" the train whistle chain three times and stops. The conductor goes to the end of the line and the next person in line becomes the new conductor.

Variation 1: Once the class understands the game, divide the class into equal-numbered groups. Each group is a train with a conductor. This gives more conductors turns in a shorter amount of time.

Variation 2: Play with multiple trains as in Variation 1. When conductors' turns are finished, have them move to the end of a different train instead of their own. Establish a rotation so conductors know which new train to go to.

Display 1: Rhythm only.

Display 2: Add solfege hint.

Display 3: Add solfege.

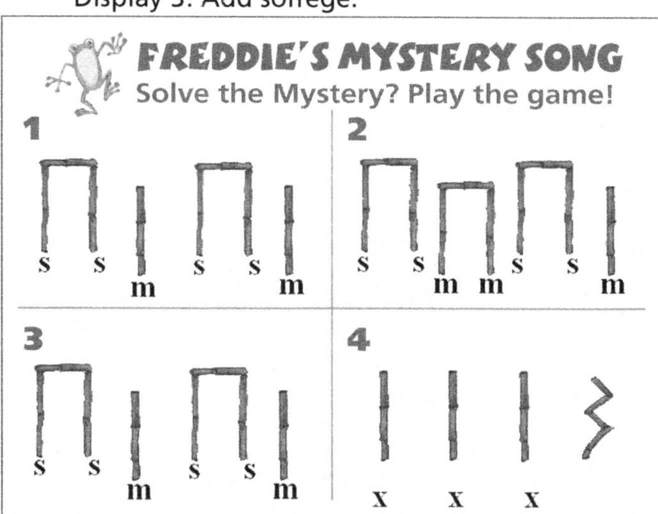

Display 4: Add lyrics.

STICKS ACTIVITY:

CHOO CHOO TRAIN

1. After playing the game, adjust the train lines into trains of four. The conductor is assigned the number 1, and the rest of the train is 2, 3, and 4 in their standing order. Place piles of sticks in front of each group.
2. Ask the students to sit on the floor where they are, count out the number of sticks they need to create the boxed pattern that matches their assigned number and "notate" it on the floor in front of them. If this is the first time doing this activity, demonstrate with one group and remember to ask leading questions of the whole class.
   - "How many sticks will it take to notate box 1?" *(Answer: 8)* Continue the questioning with box 2, 3, and 4. As they answer, each member of the demonstration group notates their assigned box (measure).
3. Sing the song while student 1 points to the first beat of his or her measure and moves left to right with the beat; student 2 takes over on his or her measure, then 3, and finally 4.
4. Ask students 1 & 2 to face each other and 3 & 4 to face each other. The odd-numbered students will be the leaders, coming up with a way to tap out the beat, and the even-numbered students will be the "mirror," mirroring how the leader is keeping the beat while singing. Switch jobs when the song repeats.
5. Switch groups. Each student stands up silently showing their number on their hand (1 finger up for "1," 2 fingers up for "2," etc.) and walks silently to another person with same number as their previous partner. Begin again from step 4 with a new partner.

PUMPKIN FAT

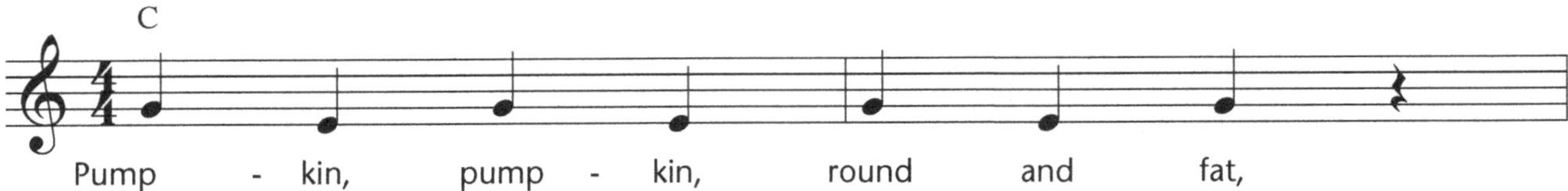

GAME

Have students stand in a circle. Pair each student with the person next to him or her and have the partners face each other.

1. In measure 1, students clap their own hands, then clap their partner's hands. Repeat.
2. In measure 2, partners join hands and form a circle with arms.
3. In measure 3, with hands still joined and in the shape of a "pumpkin," students turn their partner-circle until they are standing where their partner was just standing.
4. In measure 4, partners release their joined hands and clap and jump three times while turning back to back. On beat 4, students make a scary or silly face at the new partner they are now facing.

TEACHERS' NOTE

Students that begin facing their partner to the right will always move clockwise (to the right) when turning to a new partner. Likewise, students that begin facing their partner to the left will move counter-clockwise (to the left) when turning to a new partner.

Display 1: Rhythm only.

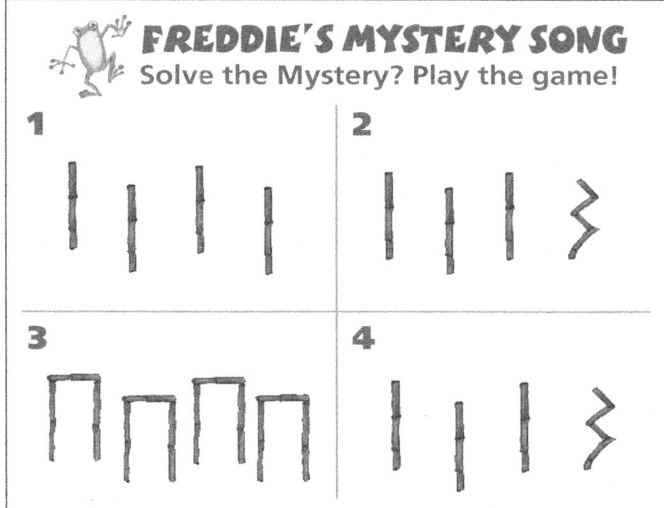

Display 2: Add solfege hint.

Display 3: Add solfege.

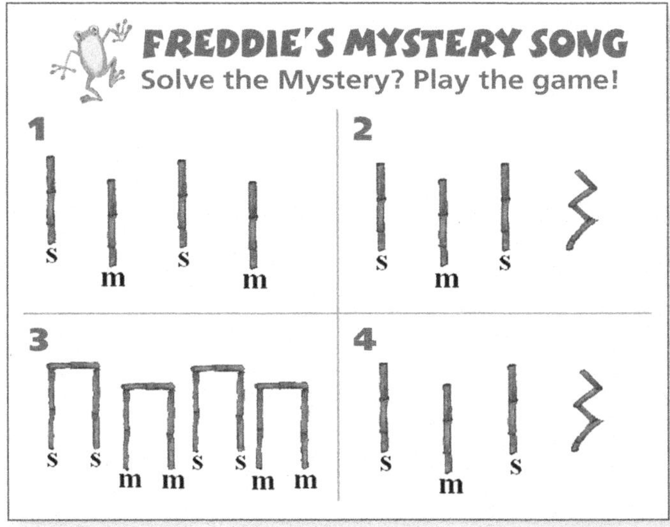

Display 4: Add lyrics.

STICKS ACTIVITY:

PUMPKIN FAT

1. After playing the game, ask students to sit on the floor with their partner. Place a pile of sticks in front of each pair.
2. Introduce the activity by asking, "How many sticks will it take to notate box 1?" *(Answer: 4)* Continue the questioning with box 2, 3, and 4. Enhance student understanding by asking, "Which boxes are alike? Which are different?"
3. Instruct each student to count out 14 sticks and work together with their partner to write the entire song on the floor.
4. Once all the partners have notated the song, have students point to the first beat of the measure and move their fingers left to right with the rhythm while singing.
5. Repeat the song until you observe each pair with the correct rhythm notation and everyone successfully pointing to the rhythm.
6. Guide the class to create new words for box 3. Sing the new song variation together.
7. Now ask the partners to create new words for box 3 on their own. Take turns sharing the variations by singing measures 1, 2, and 4 together as a class, and the chosen pair singing measure 3 on their own.

HILL HILL

GAME

1. Students stand in a line. The student who solved the Mystery Song first is the first leader. The leader faces the line.
2. Students sing the song. At the end of the song, students try to move past the leader and create a line on the other side without getting tagged by the leader.

TEACHERS' NOTE

Students can only walk. If a student breaks into a run, they sit out of the game.

Students who get tagged join the leader in tagging other students in the next round. Repeat until all students are tagged.

The last one tagged becomes the new leader and the game begins again.

Display 1: Rhythm only.

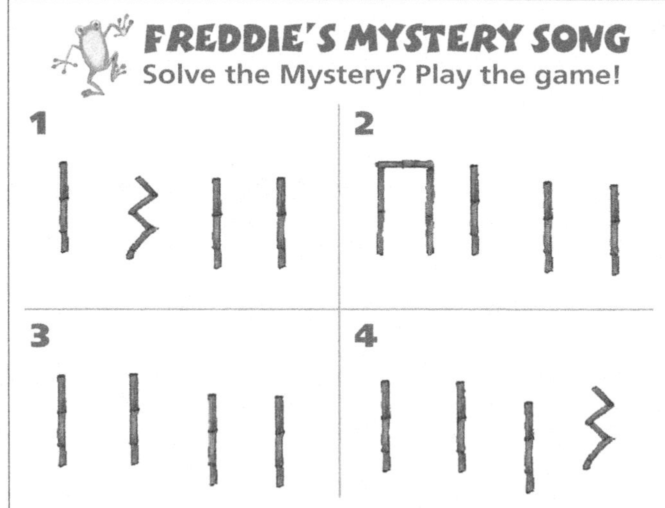

Display 2: Add solfege hint.

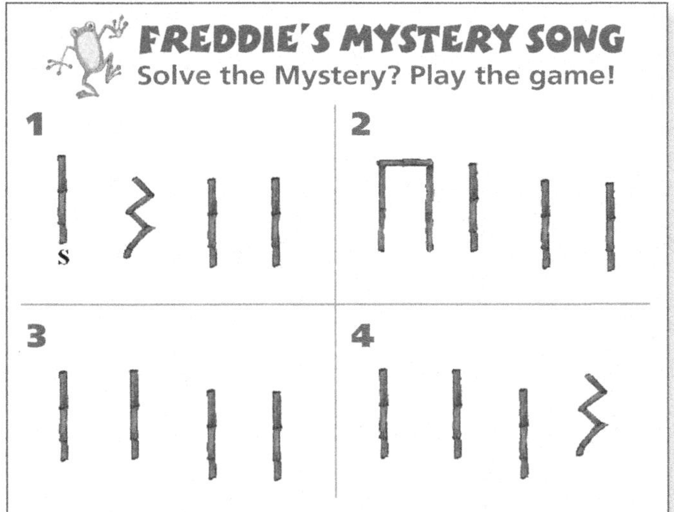

Display 3: Add solfege.

Display 4: Add lyrics.

STICKS ACTIVITY:

HILL, HILL

1. After playing the game, ask students to sit on the floor. Introduce the activity by asking, "How many sticks will it take to notate box 1?" *(Answer: 4)* Continue the questioning with box 2, 3, and 4. Enhance student understanding by asking, "Which boxes are alike? Which are different?" Ask students to count how many sticks it takes to write out the entire song. *(Answer: 22)*

2. Instruct each student to count out 22 sticks and write the song out on the floor.

3. Sing the song while students point to the first beat of the measure and move their fingers left to right with rhythm.

4. Guide the class to create a variation of the melody by changing a "sol" or "mi" to its opposite. Sing the new melodic variation together.

5. Ask for ideas of other variations and sing each one after it is suggested.

LEMONADE

GAME:

1. Students stand in two lines facing each other. Name the lines "Line 1" and "Line 2."
2. Ask the students to think of a job or trade they can act out. Tell them they need to keep it a secret. Feel free to provide an example if they seem confused.
3. Have all students pat the beat and sing the song as written below. While students are singing, walk back and forth behind one line and stop behind one student when the song ends.

   Line 1: "Here we come."

   Line 2: "Where from?"

   Line 1: "B.C."

   Line 2: "What's your trade?"

   Line 1: "Lemonade."

   Line 2: "Give us some."

   Line 1&2: "Don't be afraid."
4. The student you have stopped behind acts out a trade or a job and the students from the opposite line try to guess what it is.
5. Sing the song again and the student who just finished acting out a trade now walks behind the opposite line and chooses a new student to act out a trade at the end of the song. Continue playing as before.

Variation: Once a student's turn is finished, he or she may go to a glockenspiel and play the song while the students sing. Continue adding players on glockenspiels until everyone has had a turn.

Display 1: Rhythm only.

Display 2: Add solfege hint.

Display 3: Add solfege.

Display 4: Add lyrics.

STICKS ACTIVITY:

LEMONADE

1. After playing the game, ask students to sit on the floor with the person across from them in the opposite line. Introduce the activity by asking, "How many sticks will it take to notate box 1?" *(Answer: 6)* Continue the questioning with box 2, 3, and 4. Enhance student understanding by asking, "Which boxes are alike? Which are different?"
2. Ask students how many sticks it will take to write out the entire Lemonade song. *(Answer: 32)*
3. Have each student count out 16 sticks and work together with their partner to write the song on the floor.
4. Sing the song and have students point to the first beat of the first measure and move their fingers left to right with the rhythm.
5. Guide the class to create new call-and-response words similar to the original song. Sing the new song variation together.
6. Now ask the partners to create new lyrics similar to the original song that match the rhythm. One partner creates the call and the other creates the response. Take turns sharing the variations.

NO ROBBERS OUT TODAY

GAME

1. Students stand in two lines facing each other. The first student of each line moves to the center of the alley to become the first two "robber catchers."
2. The next students in each line become the first two "robbers." They try to sneak through the alley between the two lines without getting touched or tagged by the "robber catchers." They begin at one end of the alley. The "robber catchers'" eyes are closed and their feet cannot move.

3. Students pat the beat and sing the song while the "robber catchers" try to tag the "robbers" coming through the alley.
4. The "robber catchers" return to the line, or move to a glockenspiel to play the song while the students sing. If they go to play the glockenspiel, after playing one time they return to the lines and let the new "robber catchers" take their place playing the instruments.
5. The "robbers" become "robber catchers" and the game begins again.

TEACHERS' NOTE

The "robber catchers" must keep their eyes closed and may only bend from the waist.

Display 1: Rhythm only.

Display 2: Add solfege hint.

Display 3: Add solfege.

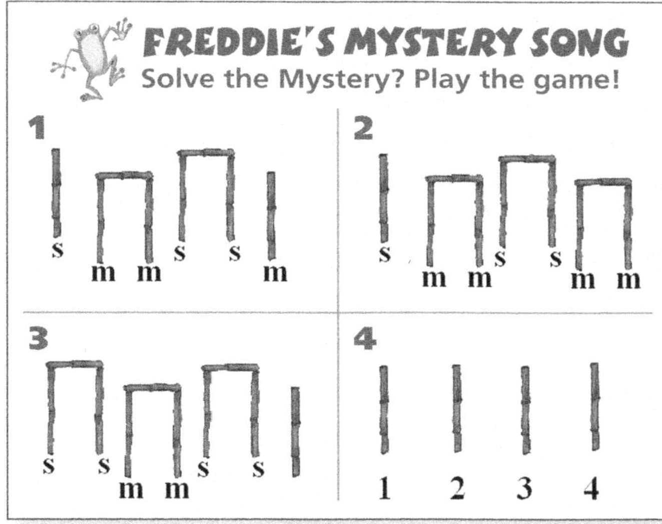

Display 4: Add lyrics.

STICKS ACTIVITY:

NO ROBBERS OUT TODAY

1. For best student understanding, analyze the song BEFORE playing the game. Ask how many sticks it takes to notate box 1 *(Answer: 8)* and continue the questioning with box 2, 3 and 4. You may also ask which boxes are alike and which are different.
2. Once students appear to understand, place one pile of sticks on a flat space near the glockenspiel or xylophone.
3. Instruct students that after their turn as a "robber catcher," they move to the sticks and write the song out while the class continues playing the game.
4. After the next round, the "robber catchers" pile their sticks back together and move to the glockenspiel to play the song while the class plays the game and the newest "robber catchers" write the song out with the sticks.
5. Students rotate again so that the first set of "robber catchers" are back in the game while the others continue to follow the rotation until everyone has a turn. Once again, the rotation goes:

   i. Start as a "Robber Catcher"
   ii. Move to notating the song with sticks
   iii. Play the glockenspiel
   iv. Return to the game

LA SOL MI MYSTERY SONGS

1. WE ARE PLAYING IN THE FOREST
2. LUCY LOCKET
3. THE MILL
4. APPLE TREE
5. SNAIL, SNAIL
6. BOUNCE HIGH
7. BELL HORSES

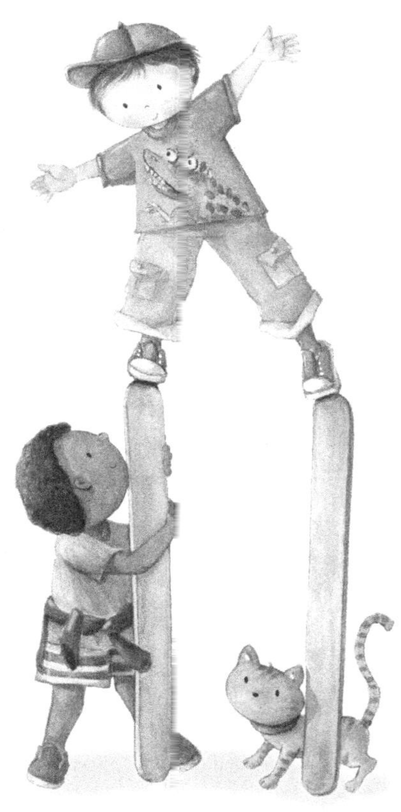

WE ARE PLAYING IN THE FOREST

INTRODUCING "LA" IN A MYSTERY SONG

1. To introduce "la" for the first time, start out by having the students chant the rhythm of a song with "la", such as "We Are Playing in the Forest", and ask if they see a pattern.
2. Ask the students, "If the first two syllables are 'sol,' what do you think the next two are?"
3. Introduce "la-la" and what it sounds like when sung. Have students echo.
4. Ask the students what letter should be put under those two notes. *(Answer: L)*
5. Have students finish telling you what letters to put underneath the other notes. If struggling, echo-sing each measure with them.
6. Ask if anyone can sing it alone, without having heard it sung by you all the way through.
7. After one student sings the song successfully, the entire class should sing the song in solfege without the teacher singing. Your class is now ready for more mystery songs that include "la."

GAME:

1. Students find their own space to stand in the classroom. Remind them that if they touch anyone, they are out of the game.
2. The student who correctly solved the mystery song at the beginning of class is the first "wolf." The "wolf" stands at the front of the room with his or her back to the rest of the students.
3. Students sing the song and continually move about in the room. As the song ends, the students freeze and the "wolf" turns quickly around to try to catch anyone still moving. If the "wolf" sees anyone move (with exceptions, of course, for blinking and breathing), the "wolf" says the student's name and the student has to sit in his or her seat.
4. Each "wolf" gets two rounds to be the "wolf." All students who were caught moving are back in the game with each new "wolf." This way, a student is only "out" for one round maximum.

Display 1: Rhythm only.

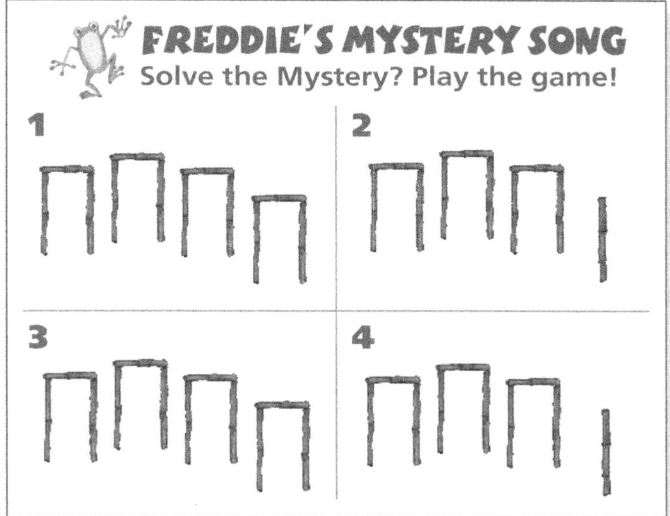

Display 2: Add solfege hint.

Display 3: Add solfege.

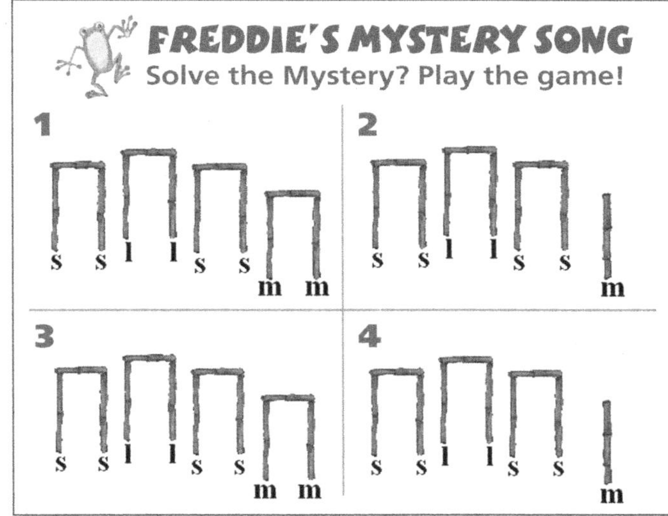

Display 4: Add lyrics.

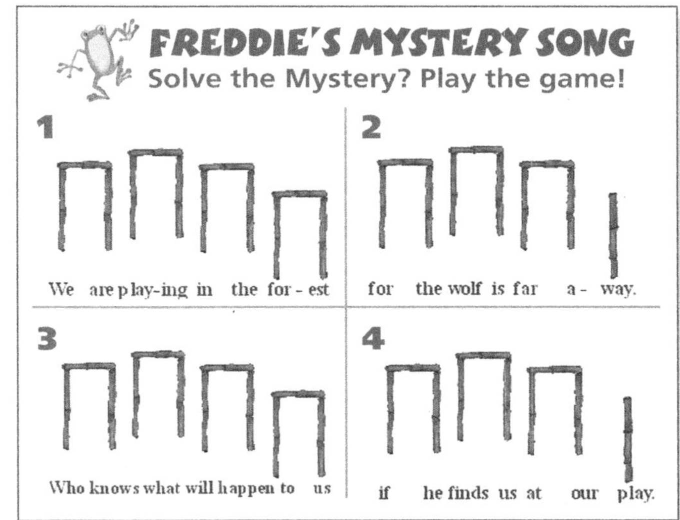

STICKS ACTIVITY:

WE ARE PLAYING IN THE FOREST

1. After playing one round of the game, ask the kids to sit on the floor.
2. Ask students, "How many sticks will it take to notate box 1?" *(Answer: 12)* Continue the questioning with boxes 2, 3, and 4. Ask them which boxes are alike and which are different and encourage them to describe the differences to you. Have students tell you how many sticks it takes to write the first two boxes of the song. *(Answer: 22)*
3. Work together as a class to write the first two measures of the song with sticks on the floor near a glockenspiel or other barred instrument or piano.
4. Sing the song pointing to the first beat of the measure and moving left to right while singing. To complete the song, students will go through the pattern twice.
5. Demonstrate playing the song on the pitched instrument. Invite the student who just finished being "the wolf" to play on the pitched instrument while the class plays the game with a new "wolf."
6. Each time a "wolf" is finished with his or her turn, he or she takes a turn playing the pitched instrument before returning to the game.

STICKS!

LUCY LOCKET

GAME:

1. Have students stand in a circle. Place a variety of rhythm instruments in the middle of the circle.
2. Display a "pocket," or little purse, to the class. Inside the "pocket," place miniature 4-beat rhythm pattern cards. Alternatively, you may use any object and just pretend that it is Lucy's Pocket. Craft stores often sell small nylon bags with drawstring ribbon that work perfectly.
3. Pass the object designated as Lucy's Pocket around the circle to the beat of the song while singing. Whoever has the pocket at the end of the song, opens it, pulls out a rhythm card and chants it while the other students pat the beat on their upper thighs.
4. The students continue to pat the beat while the one student goes to a rhythm instrument in the center of the circle and plays the pattern two times.
5. The student replaces the rhythm card in the pocket, returns to the circle, and the game begins again.

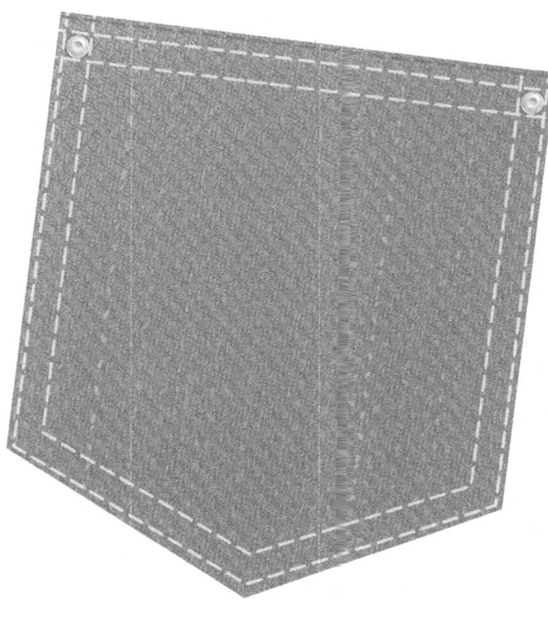

Display 1: Rhythm only.

Display 2: Add solfege hint.

Display 3: Add solfege.

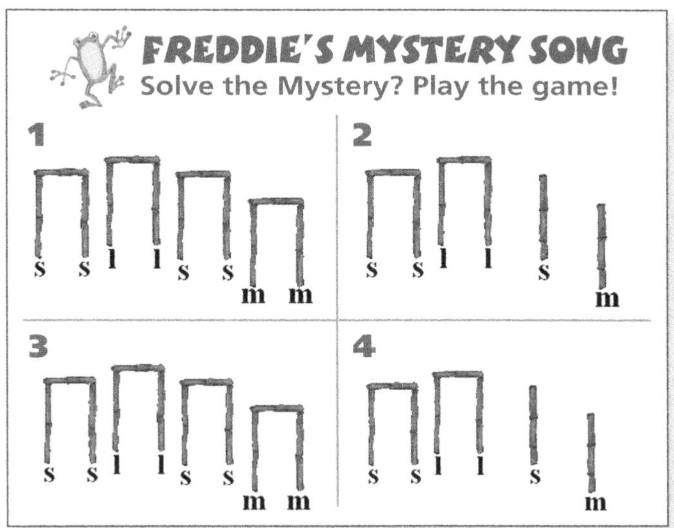

Display 4: Add lyrics.

STICKS ACTIVITY:

LUCY LOCKET

1. After playing one round of the game, ask the kids to sit on the floor in the circle.
2. Ask students to tell you how many sticks it takes to notate box 1. *(Answer: 12)* Continue questioning with box 2, 3, and 4.
3. Work together as a class to write the song with sticks on the floor inside the circle near a glockenspiel or other barred instrument. Play on the instrument.
4. Ask the student currently holding Lucy's Pocket to pull out one rhythm pattern and chant it. Have the other students echo.
5. The student who chose the card should now write the rhythm using sticks and play it on the glockenspiel.
6. Play the game again and give student who just played the choice to either accompany the class on the instrument during the next round or return to the circle.
7. Repeat the pattern with the next student who ends up with Lucy's Pocket.

THE MILL

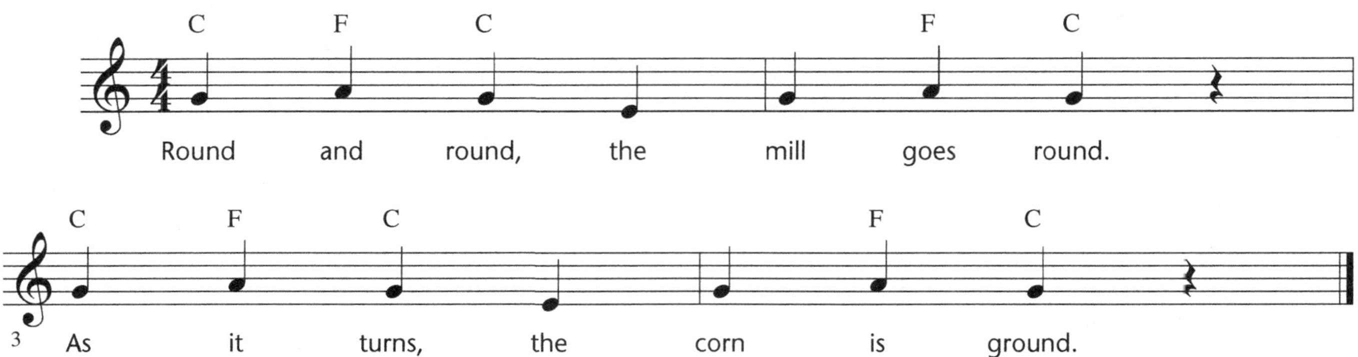

GAME:

1. Students stand in a circle facing the left, ready to walk clockwise.
2. One student is the "miller." The "miller" stands outside the circle facing the right, ready to walk counter-clockwise.
3. Students begin to sing the song and walk in their respective directions.
4. Whoever "the miller" is standing next to on the last word of the song is "ground" and becomes a second "miller" for the next round.
5. As the second round ends, there will be two more students "ground" and added to the group of "millers."
6. Each round, the number of students "ground" and made "millers" doubles until only one or none are left.
7. The last student left becomes the new first "miller" and the game begins again.

Variation 1: For younger students, the first "miller" chooses one student to "ground" and the "ground" student must sit out and/or keep the beat on his or her lap or a rhythm instrument. Keep repeating until there is only one person left "un-ground."

Variation 2: Once a student has a turn being the "miller," he or she goes to a glockenspiel and plays the melody while the game continues. In this variation, one "miller" is always on the outside of the circle with multiple students playing a glockenspiel to accompany the song.

Display 1: Rhythm only.

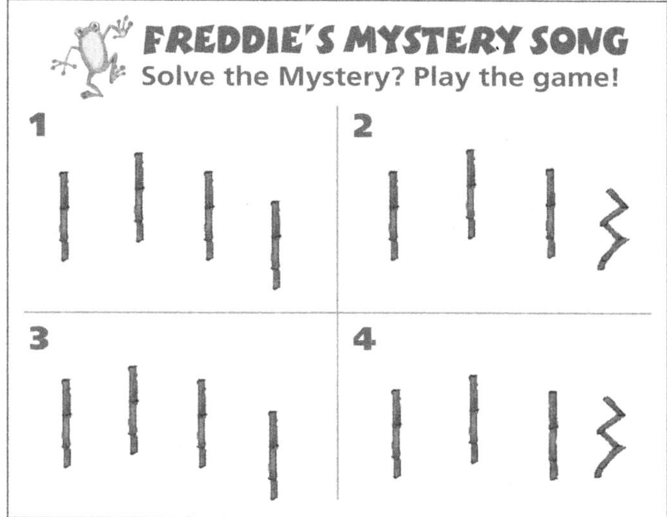

Display 2: Add solfege hint.

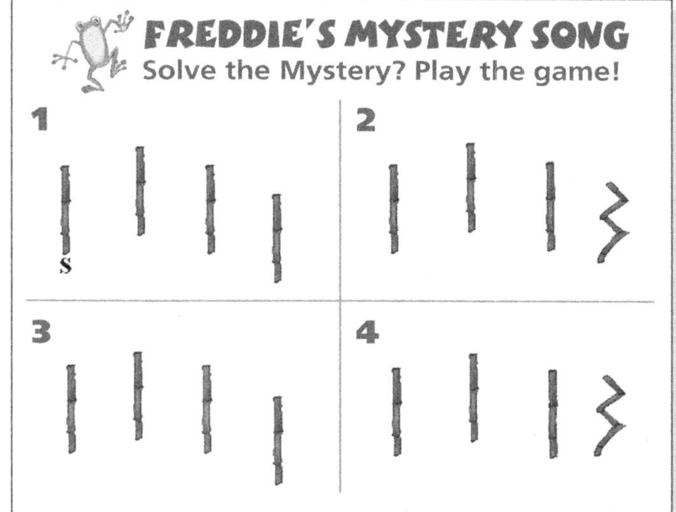

Display 3: Add solfege.

Display 4: Add lyrics.

STICKS ACTIVITY:

THE MILL

1. After playing one round of the game, ask the students to sit on the floor. Have students tell you how many sticks will it take to notate box. *(Answer: 4)* Continue the questioning with box 2, 3, and 4.
2. Ask students how many sticks it will take to write the first two boxes of the song. *(Answer: 10)* Encourage them to use addition by asking, "Since the pattern repeats, what can you add to know how many sticks it takes to write the whole song?" *(Answer: 10+10=20)*
3. Work together as a class to write the whole song with sticks on the floor near a glockenspiel or other barred instrument. Sing the song while pointing to the first beat of the measure and moving left to right with the rhythm.
4. Demonstrate playing the song on the pitched instrument. Invite the student who just finished being "the miller" to play on the pitched instrument while the class plays the game with the student who was "ground" as the new "miller." Rotate turns.

APPLE TREE

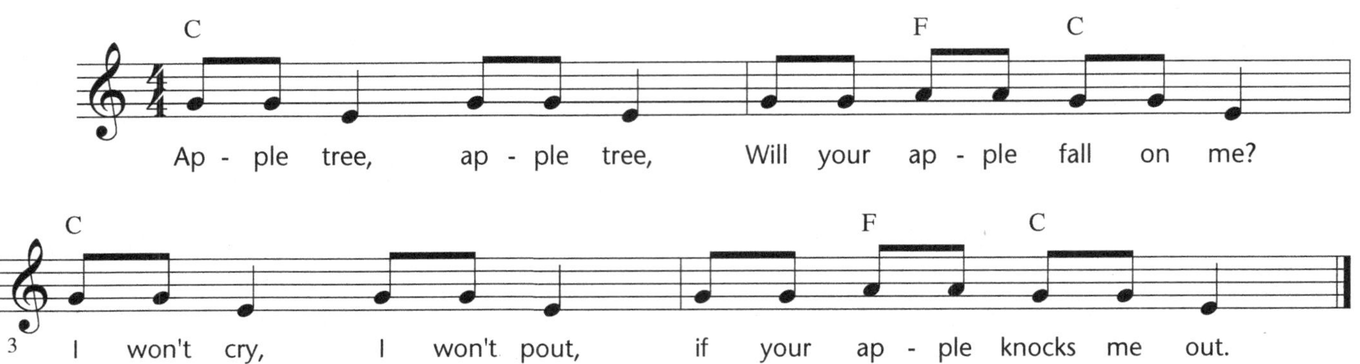

GAME:

1. Students begin by standing in a line, ready to follow the leader.
2. Stand with your arms up and stretched in front of you like two tree branches extended above a road. You are the "apple tree."
3. Students begin to walk under the "branches" (your arms) and around in a large circle to walk under the branches again. Continue to walk until the last word of the song.
4. On the last word, the students freeze and the "apple tree" points down at the student currently standing beneath the branches and says their name. The fingers are the "leaves" on the branch, pointing to the one that is now "out." (By doing this, you can eliminate dropping the arms down and capturing kids. If students drop their branches when they are the "apple tree," they must sit out of the game.)

5. Whoever is "out" at the end of the round becomes another "tree" opposite the first "tree," forming an alley.
6. The game continues but the next student to be "out" becomes a "tree" on the opposite side of the room, forming a natural circle as the students are forced to go under two trees on the opposite side of the room.
7. As students get "out" under multiple trees, they continue to create new pairs of "trees" across the room from each other in the shape of a circle. The last student left gets to run through the alley while the "apple trees" sing the song one last time.

Display 1: Rhythm only.

Display 2: Add solfege hint.

Display 3: Add solfege.

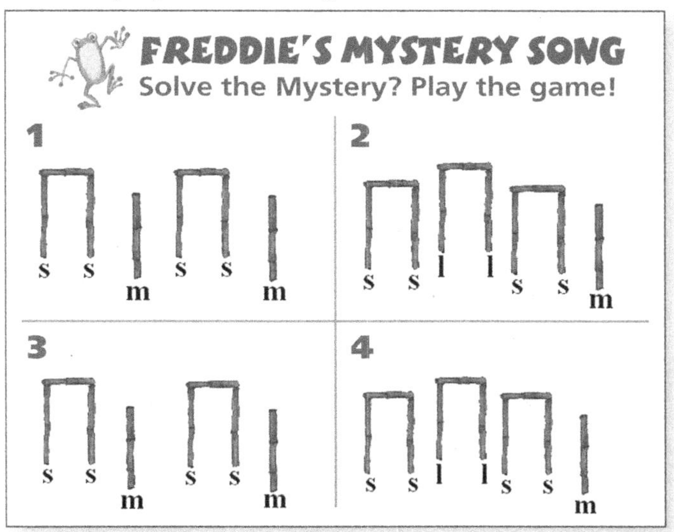

Display 4: Add lyrics.

STICKS ACTIVITY:

APPLE TREE

1. After playing the game, have the students sit on the floor with their "tree" partner.
2. Ask them how many sticks it will take to notate box 1. *(Answer: 8)* Continue the questioning with box 2, 3, and 4.
3. Ask students how many sticks it will take to write the first two boxes of the song. *(Answer: 18)* Encourage them to use addition by asking, "Since the pattern repeats, what can you add to know how many sticks it takes to write the whole song?" *(Answer: 18+18=36)*
4. Have the partners each count out 18 sticks and work together to write the song. Sing the song while pointing to the first beat of the first measure and moving left to right with the rhythm.
5. Have the students work together in their pairs to create new lyrics for at least one box. However, the words in Box 1 should stay the same.
6. Share the variations with the class. Silliness welcome!

STICKS!

SNAIL, SNAIL

GAME:

1. Students form a line and hold hands with the person next to them.
2. One student at the end is the leader and leads the line into a spiraling circle and then unwinds them back to a regular circular. This creates a snail shell shape.
3. You may want to have them practice this while you sing the song the first few times.
4. Students should be sure to step to the beat of the music. This game is "magical" for kids!

Display 1: Rhythm only.

Display 2: Add solfege hint.

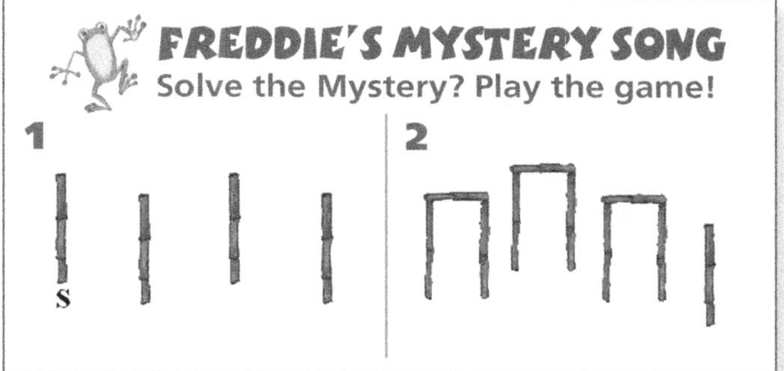

Display 3: Add solfege.

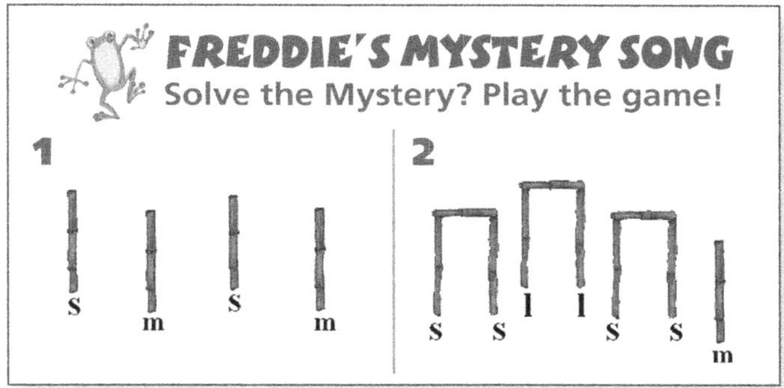

Display 4: Add lyrics.

STICKS ACTIVITY:

SNAIL, SNAIL

1. After playing the game, ask the students to sit on the floor and to tell you how many sticks it will take to notate the song. *(Answer: 14)*
2. Have each student count out 14 sticks and notate the song on the floor. Sing the song while pointing to the first beat and moving left to right with the rhythm.
3. Ask the students, "How could we change the melody?" Guide them in changing one thing, such as making the first measure read, "sol, sol, sol, mi."
4. Sing the melodic variation. Have your students echo.
5. Invite more creative variations of the melody and echo sing the changes.
6. After a few demonstrations, invite the students to try solo singing what they think their suggested change will sound like.

BOUNCE HIGH

GAME:

1. Have students stand in a circle. Bounce a ball across the circle to a student. The student should bounce the ball back to you while the class sings the song. Bounce the ball to a different student and repeat.

2. Try to bounce the ball on beats 1 & 3.

Variation 1: Ask the students what other places they could go that end with an "o", such as Ohio, Costco, etc. Change the last word and continue playing.

Variation 2: Students bounce to a new person instead of back to the teacher.

Variation 3: The student with the ball bounces it up and down for four beats while he or she thinks about to whom to bounce the ball in the second measure. All students sing the first measure; the student with the ball sings the second measure solo, inserting the name of their chosen person with an added "o" at the end as he or she bounces it. For example, if the student chooses to bounce the ball to another student named "John," the student bouncing the ball would sing,"... bounce the ball to John-i-o!"

Display 1: Rhythm only.

FREDDIE'S MYSTERY SONG
Solve the Mystery? Play the game!
1
2

Display 2: Add solfege hint.

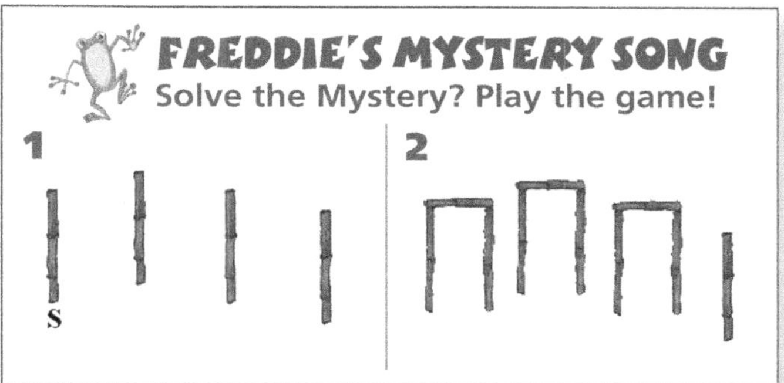

Display 3: Add solfege.

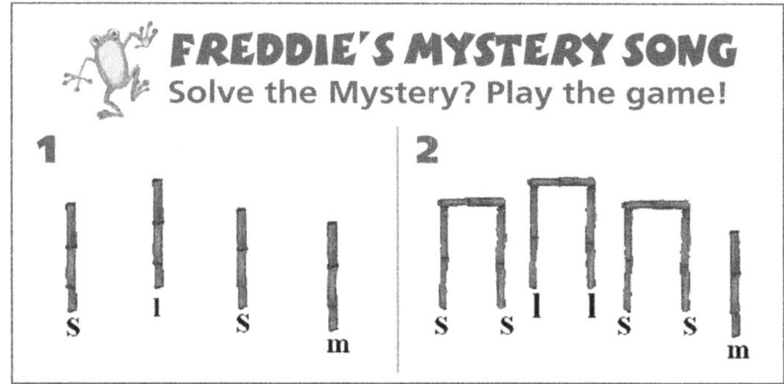

Display 4: Add lyrics.

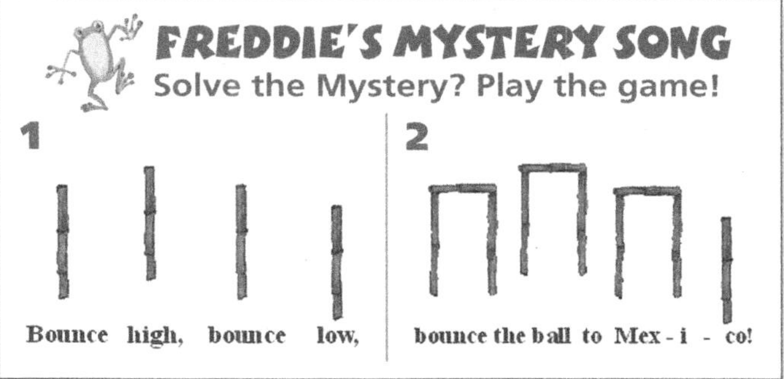

STICKS ACTIVITY:

BOUNCE HIGH

1. After playing the game, ask the students to sit on the floor and tell you how many sticks it takes to notate the song. *(Answer: 14)*
2. Each student counts out 14 sticks and writes out the song. Sing the song while pointing to the first beat and moving left to right with the rhythm.
3. As in Variation 1 of the game, ask the students to come up with new places to go that end in "o."
4. Encourage students to come up with melodic variations. Sing the suggested variations and have students echo.
5. After a few demonstrations, invite the students to try solo singing what they think their suggested change will sound like.

STICKS!

BELL HORSES

GAME:

1. Establish a "race course." It can be straight across the room, in a circular pattern like a racetrack, or whatever works best for your situation. The person who solved the mystery song first gets to choose one or two other students to be "horses" with them.
2. The two or three "horses" line up at the starting line and prepare to race.
3. The students not racing sing the song. On the last beat of the song, say "Go!" and the students begin to race by galloping like a horse from beginning to end.
4. The first one to cross the finish line gets to choose one or two new "horses" and race again.

Display 1: Rhythm only.

Display 2: Add solfege hint.

Display 3: Add solfege.

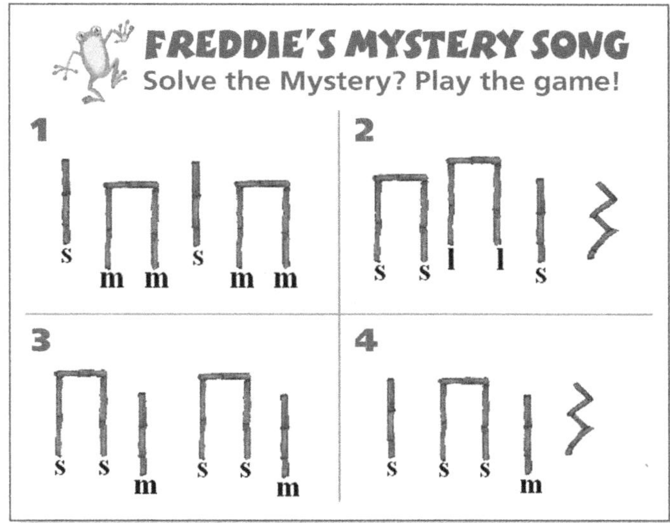

Display 4: Add lyrics.

STICKS ACTIVITY:

BELL HORSES

1. Before playing the game, ask the students how many sticks it will take to notate box 1. *(Answer: 8)* Continue the questioning with box 2, 3, and 4.
2. Work together as a class to write the song with sticks on the floor near glockenspiels or other barred instruments. (If possible, have enough instruments for all to use.) Sing the song while pointing to the first beat and moving left to right with the rhythm.
3. Demonstrate playing the song on a pitched instrument. Ask the students to play the song on their instrument. Tell them you are watching for three students doing their job and playing well to get a turn in the horse race.
4. Choose three students to be the "horses" as described in the game. Other students play and sing as the horses prepare to race. Race begins at the end of the song.
5. Pick three new students to race while others play the song. Remind them that you are picking students who are doing their job and playing well. This keeps the kids on task amid the excitement. They want a chance to be in the horse race!

MI RE DO MYSTERY SONGS

1. HOT CROSS BUNS
2. CLOSET KEY

INTRODUCING "DO" AND "RE" IN A MYSTERY SONG

1. Have students chant the rhythm of the song and ask if they see a pattern. They should be able to tell you which boxes are the same and which are different.
2. Ask students, "If the first syllable is 'mi,' what do you think the next two are?"
3. Introduce "re" and "do" and what they sound like when sung. Have students echo.
4. Ask students what letters should be written under the notes in box 3. *(Answer: D for the first four and R for that last four)* Have them tell you how to fill in the rest of the letters. Echo sing each box if students are struggling for accuracy.
5. Ask if anyone can sing it alone, without having heard it sung by you all the way through. After one student sings the song successfully, the entire class should sing the song in solfege without the teacher singing.
6. Once the song is sung successfully, your class is ready for the last step. Ask if anyone recognizes the singing game. Guide them to the answer if they need help.
7. Sing the lyrics and play the game!

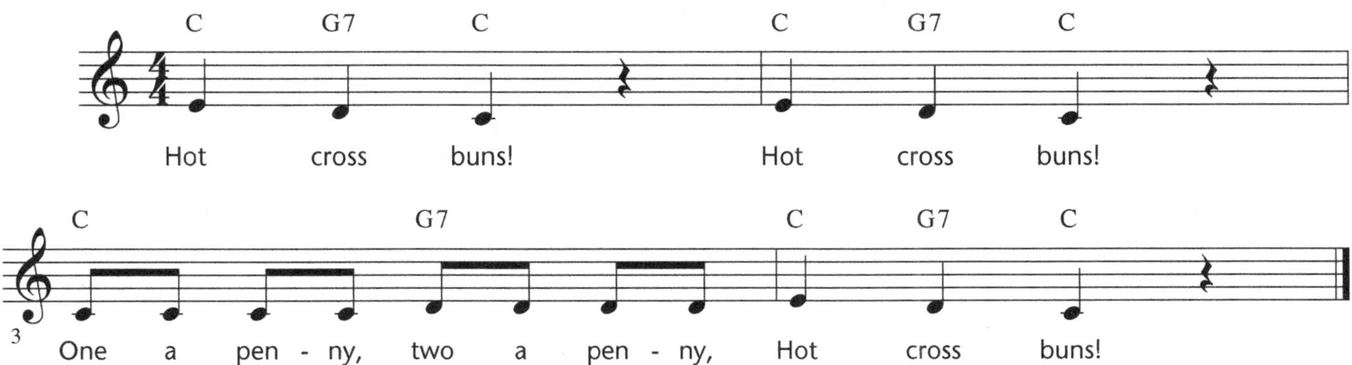

GAME:

1. Students stand in a circle. Pair each student with the person next to him or her and have the partners face each other. One partner will be facing the left, ready to move clockwise. The other will be facing the right, ready to move counter-clockwise.
2. In measures 1 and 2, partners clap their own hands, cross their arms onto their own shoulders, then clap their partner's hands. All this should be done to the beat of the song.
3. In measure 3, move forward with tip-toe running steps in time to the eighth note rhythm pattern until standing in their partner's place, face-to-face with a new partner.
4. In measure 4, repeat the clapping pattern from measures 1 and 2 with the new partner.

Variation: Sing in solfege and play again. Replace hand signs for the clapping pattern.

TEACHERS' NOTE

Partners that begin facing clockwise, will always move clockwise around the circle to a new partner. Likewise, partners facing counter-clockwise will always move counter-clockwise until they reach their original partner.

Display 1: Rhythm only.

Display 2: Add solfege hint.

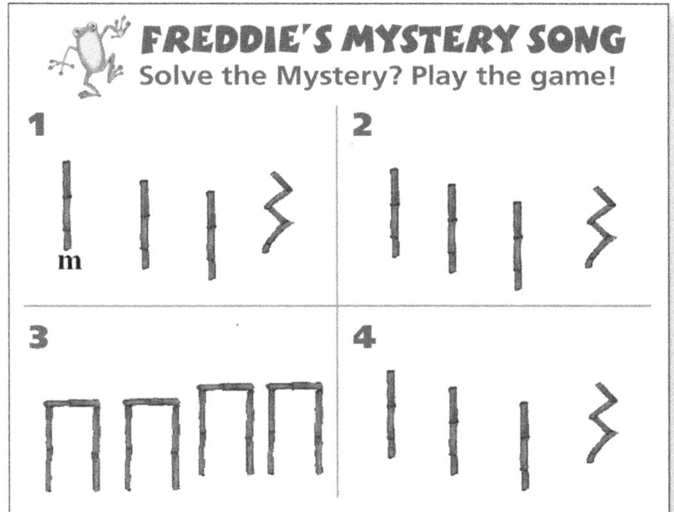

Display 3: Add solfege.

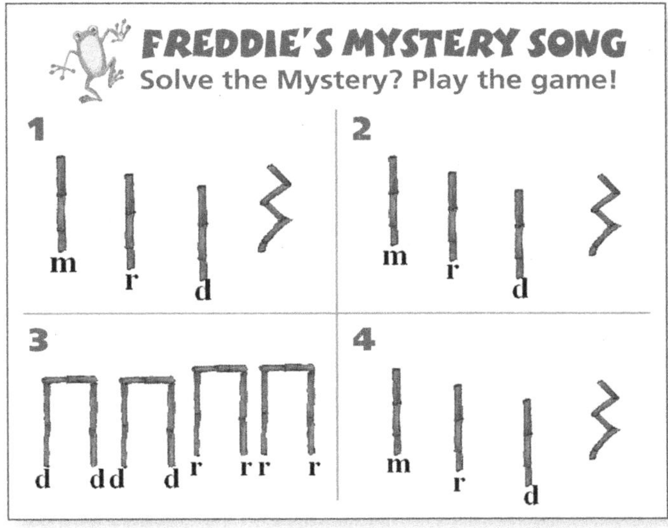

Display 4: Add lyrics.

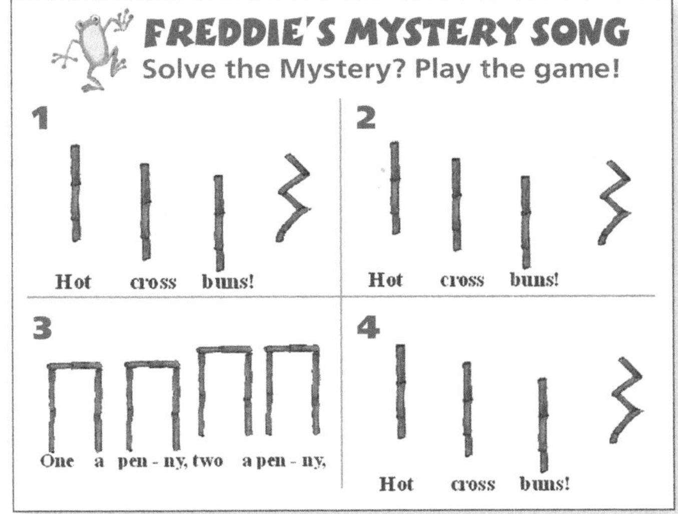

STICKS ACTIVITY:

HOT CROSS BUNS

1. After playing one round of the game, ask the kids to sit on the floor beside their partner.
2. Ask students how many sticks it will take to notate box 1. *(Answer: 6)* Continue the questioning with boxes 2, 3, and 4.
3. Ask students how many sticks it will take to write the whole song. *(Answer: 30)* You may want to ask, "What is half of 30?" to help them answer this question: "How many sticks will you and your partner each need to write the whole song?" *(Answer: 15)*
4. Partners work together to write the song with sticks on the floor near a glockenspiel or other barred instrument. Partners will share an instrument.
5. Demonstrate playing the song on a pitched instrument. Guide the students in playing and singing the song together.
6. Ask the partners to create new words, or lyrics, for the song. The lyrics have to match the existing rhythm and melody.
7. Have the class play their instruments while one set of partners sing their variation. Continue taking turns sharing while the class plays.

CLOSET KEY

GAME:

1. Send one student to a corner of the room to close and cover his or her eyes.
2. Another student is given a physical key to hide anywhere in the room. At least a piece of the key needs to be showing. When the key has been hidden, that student may return to his or her seat and the student covering his or her eyes may open them.
3. The only clue given to the student who must find the key is the class' singing voices. If the student is far away from the hiding place, the class sings softly. As he or she moves closer to the key, the class sings louder.
4. Once the student realizes she or he is getting close, announce "Level 2." In "Level 2", the class will sing loudly or softly based on whether the student is looking in the right direction of the hiding spot or not. The round ends once the key is found.
5. Two new players get a turn to hide and find the key.

FREDDIE THE FROG® BOOKS AND MATERIALS REFERENCED IN THIS BOOK

Freddie the Frog and the Mysterious Wahooooo Book/Audio CD (HL09971503)

Tempo Island Magnetic Rhythm Board Set (HL09971504)

OTHER FREDDIE THE FROG® MATERIALS

Beyond the Books: Teaching Tips, Tools and Assessment (HL35027959)

www.FreddieTheFrog.com

Find Internet games and coloring pages that reinforce musical concepts. And don't miss the Freddie the Frog® iPad App!